Angkor Wat
Archaeological Park

ANTON SWANEPOEL

**The Ultimate Guide To exploring
Angkor Wat Archaeological Park
and its timeless treasures.**

AntonSwanepoel
www.antonswanepoelbooks.com

Anton Swanepoel

http://antonswanepoelbooks.com/
http://antonswanepoelbooks.com/blog/
http://www.facebook.com/AuthorAntonSwanepoel
https://twitter.com/Author_Anton

Follow this link if you want updates on new book releases by the
Author. http://antonswanepoelbooks.com/subscribe.php
For travel tips follow his blog.

Introduction

Magical Angkor Wat temple amazes more than 2 million visitors each year. However, there are more than 700 temples scattered around Angkor Wat and the nearby mountains and towns, with more than 50 temples in the Angkor Archaeological Park alone.

This book contains over 380 pictures, and covers 50 temples and attractions in the Angkor Wat Archaeological Park, as well as an additional 15 surrounding temples or attractions. Additionally included are the five gates found in the park.

This book is intended for visitors that have a bit more time and want to see hidden and not often visited temples, such as Mangalartha Temple and Prasat Chrung. Alternatively, people that want to see how the temples look like that they may not be able to visit, will find this book of interest. Note; this book is an extended version of my smaller book, **Angkor Wat Temples**, which contains over 250 pictures, and covers over 30 temples in the Angkor Archaeological Park.

All temples have gps coordinates that allows you to find them easily yourself. In the back of the book, you will find a map of Angkor Wat Archaeological Park, as well as a link for a larger map that shows the location of the Roluos group of temples and more.

The temples in the park are listed in order, as you would find them when going around either the small or grand circuit.

For visitors that have only a day or two in Siem Reap and are only interested in the top temples, then **Angkor Wat: 20 Must See Temples**, may be of interest.

If you are visiting other parts of Cambodia, see my books about the other towns. **http://antonswanepoelbooks.com/cambodia.php**

Table of Contents

Chapter 1: How much time

This book contains information on a total of 71 attractions. To see them all, would require around 4 to 6 days. The following times are from my experience in visiting these temples and living in Cambodia for 18 months.

A full one-day visit from 5:30am to 5:30pm allows you to see the highlights of Angkor Wat, Bayon, Baphuon, the Elephant and Leper King terraces, Ta Prohm, and possibly Phnom Bakheng, but very little else.

A three-day visit allows you to see the major temples and some minor temples once.

Seven days allows you to see all the temples listed in this book under Angkor Archaeological Park once, with a second visit to the larger temples, while also seeing Kbal Spean and Kulen Mountain.

Two weeks (fast passed, three weeks suggested) will allow you to see all the temples and attraction in the Angkor Archaeological Park, with all the temples and attractions listed in Siem Reap, plus allow you to see Kbal Spean , Kulen Mountain, Chau Srei Vibol, Banteay Chhmar, as well as Koh Ker temple complex, Preah Vihear Temple and Anlong Ven.

If you are interested in seeing all these attractions, then my larger book, **Angkor Wat & Cambodia Temples** is suggested. If you are only interested in some of the additional attractions, then see the books about those attractions on my website.

Chapter 2: Khmer Kings

Following are Khmer rulers, and the temples they are known to have built or made additions or restorations to.

Isanavarman I 611 ~ 635
Sambor Preikuk Temple Site.

Jayavarman II 790 ~ 835
Rong Chen (Phnom Kulen), early structure at Kutisvara.

Jayavarman III 835 ~ 877
Prei Monti, Trapeang Phong, Bakong.

Indravarman I 877 – c.886
Preah Ko, Sandstone additions to Bakong, Indratataka Baray (Baray at Roluos group that Prasat Lolei is situated in).

Yasovarman I 889 – c.915
Prasat Lolei, Bakheng, Prasat Bei, Thma Bay Kaek, early structure at Phimeanakas, Phnom Krom, Phnom Bok, East Baray.

Harshavarman I c.915 ~ 923
Baksei Chamkrong, Prasat Kravan.

Isanavarman II 923 – c.928
None known.

Jayavarman IV c.928 – c.941
Koh Ker temple site.

Harshavarman II c.941 ~ 944
None Known.

Rajendravarman 944 ~ 968
Pre Rup, East Mebon, Bat Chum, Kutisvara, Banteay Srei. Earlier temple on the site of Banteay Kdei, Srah Srang, Baksei Chamkrong.

Jayavarman V 968 ~ 1000
Ta Keo.

Udayadityavarman I 1001 ~ 1002
None Known.

Jayaviravarman 1002 ~ 1010
North Khleang, additions to Ta Keo.

Suryavarman I 1002 ~ 1049
South Khleang, Preah Vihear in the Dangrek Mountains, Phimeanakas, Royal Palace, Suryaparvata at Phnom Chisor, Preah Khan at Kompong Svay, West Baray, Wat Phu.

Udayadityavarman II 1050 ~ 1066
Baphuon, West Mebon.

Harshavarman III 1066/7~1080
None known.

Jayavarman VI 1080 ~ c.1107
Phimai in present-day Thailand

Dharanindravarman I 1107 ~ 1112
None Known.

Suryavarman II 1113 ~ c.1150
Angkor Wat, Thommanon, Chao Say Tevoda, Banteay Samre, Phnom Rung in present—day Thailand, Beng Mealea.

Yasovarman II c.1150~1165
Beng Mealea, Chao Say Tevoda, Banteay Samre, Bakong.

Tribhuvanadityavarman c.1165~1177
None Known.

Jayavarman VII 1181 ~ c.1220
Ta Prohm, Preah Khan, Jayatataka baray (baray Neak Pean is in), Neak Pean, Ta Som, Ta Nei, Banteay Chhmar, Angkor Thom, the four Prasat Chrungs (structures in the four corners of Angkor Thom City) Bayon, Elephant Terrace, Ta Prohm Kel, Hospital Chapel, Krol Ko, Srah Srang, Royal Palace.

Indravarman II c.1220 – 1243
Prasats Suor Prat, Ta Prohm, Banteay Kdei, Ta Som, Ta Nei.

Jayavarman VIII c.1243 ~ 1295
Mangalartha, Preah Palilay (debated), Bayon, Ta Prohm, Preah Khan, Prasat Chrungs (structures in the four corners of Angkor Thom City), Angkor Wat, Baphuon, Chao Say Tevoda, Banteay Samre, Beng Mealea, Terrace of the Leper King, Elephant Terrace, Preah Pithu, Royal Palace.

Srindravarman 1295~1307
Ta Prohm, Preah Pithu, Preah Palilay.

Srindrajayavarman 1307~1327
None known.

Jayavarman Paramesvara 1327 ~ unknown.
None known.

Chapter 3: Angkor Archaeological Park

Angkor Archaeological Park stretches over 400 square km and contains some of the most magnificent temple remains of several capitals of the Khmer Empire that lasted from the 9th to the 15th century. The park is around 5km from the nearby town, Siem Reap, and was declared a UNESCO World Heritage site in 1992. The complex houses over 70 temples and sights, of which 63 are covered in this book. Both Buddhism and Hindu temples are found in the park, with many altered from Buddhism to Hindu, when the religion changed in the 13th century, with some changed back to Buddhism later.

The Angkorian period began in 790 when Jayavarman II became king. He established his capital in Hariharalaya, near the Roluos group temples. He later, after military setbacks, moved his capital to the Kulen Mountains, where in 802, he declared himself a God-King, and World-Emperor. The Angkor area continued to grow through the times, until 1431, when a rebellion led by Ayutthaya sacked Angkor, and caused the population to abandon the temples.

Entry pass office

All visitors to the park must have a photo id entry pass that is issued at the office just before entering the park. Passes are checked at every temple, and large fines are given for people not having an entry pass. Note that most temples close to the park, such as Banteay Srei, Banteay Samre, and the Roluos group, require you to have an Angkor Pass. Thus, if you want to visit these temples, get your pass before you head out to the temples. Outer temples such as Koh Ker, Ben Mealea, have their own entry pass office. See entry requirements at the start of each chapter to make sure, before you go. Do note that the rules do change without notice, so it is advised to ask your tuk tuk driver for requirements before you head out. The office is on Charles De Gualle Street, 2.8km from the crossing with national road 6.

GPS: 13°23'12.7"N 103°51'50.6"E.
$60 for 7 entries, valid for one month.
$40 for 3 entries, valid for one week.
$20 for a day.
Entry for Cambodians and children under 12 years old are free.

Open: 5:00am ~ 5:30pm for passes office. 5:30am ~ 5:30pm for temples.

Ticket office on the way to the Angkor Archaeological Park.

Note, an Angkor ticket is required for Banteay Srei, The Roluos Group, Kbal Spean, Banteay Samre, and Phnom Krom. There are no entry pass offices at these temples; you have to get your Angkor Pass before you go to these temples. You will not be allowed in, without a pass.

Note, most of the time a pass for Phnom Krom was not required when I visited, but I have at times (normally festivals), been asked for one. Passes for Beng Mealea, Koh Ker, Kulen Mountain, landmine museum, museum, Tonle Sap Lake and war museum, are sold at or before you get to these places. At current, a pass for Ak Yum, Prei Monti, Prasat To, West Mebon and Phnom Bok is not required, but this may change without notice. Always check before heading out to the temples.

Note, rules as of Dec 2014. Passes are not refundable, nor transferable. Unused entries are lost when the pass expires. Lost passes cannot be replaced, and damaged passes (date and picture cannot be read, is laminated by you, or has gotten wet) are not valid. Passes are checked at every temple entrance, and a large fine is issued if you have no valid pass inside the Angkor Park. You can only buy a one-day pass for the next day, after 5pm. Children under 12 years old are free, **if they have their passport with them.**

Gates

There are five main gates in the Angkor Archaeological Park, with the South and Victory gates used the most frequently, followed by the North Gate. The East and West gates are mostly used by locals. The gates are built in similar style, with figures on them. There are small rooms inside the walls on either side of the opening of the gates.

East Gate

Time: 20 minutes.
GPS: 13°26'28.4"N 103°51'39.2"E for the road leading to the gate.
GPS: 13°26'28.9"N 103°52'21.4"E for the gate.

The East gate is 1.3km down a dirt road, leading from the east side of Bayon Temple (where the temple is furthest from the road). From Angkor Wat, turn right as you get to Bayon, follow the road around to the first entrance, and then turn right down a dirt path directly opposite the entrance. The road to the temple itself is worth a walk or cycle if you have the time. The gate is mostly unvisited, and with the ground next to the gate, allowing one to get closer to the faces on the gate, it makes for a good photo opportunity.

Anton Swanepoel

North Gate

Time: 20 minutes.
GPS: 13°27'19.1"N 103°51'32.2"E.

The North gate is 850m from the Leaper King Terraces, with the Terraces on your left. The gate offers the opportunity to climb the incline next to the gate, and get closer pictures of the faces on the gates.

South Gate

Time: 15 to 45 minutes.
GPS: 13°25'35.3"N 103°51'34.9"E.

The South gate is 1.5km from the main Angkor Wat Temple entrance, and is the busiest gate. The South Gate has a large bridge, and offers very good views of the river from it.

If you travel from Angkor Wat Temple to Bayon, you will use this gate. It is also the route and gate used by the elephant tours. Boat tickets to ride the Angkor Thom City Moat, are sold on the left of the bridge, just before you get to the bridge and gate, as coming from Angkor Wat Temple.

The figures on the sides of the bridge are 54 Hindu deities (left side) and 54 Demons or Asuras (right side), that each carries a seven headed Vasuki Naga (King of the Naga's).

Victory Gate

Time: 15 minutes.
GPS: 13°26'45.6"N 103°52'21.9"E.

Victory Gate is on the small circuit route, and 600m from the East Gate, and 1.5km from the Elephant Terrace. The road to the gate leads away from the Elephant terrace, and passes between the North and South Preah Pithu towers. A side road a short distance from both gates links the East and Victory gate. Like other gates, you can climb up.

Anton Swanepoel

West Gate

Time: 15 minutes.
GPS: 13°26'28.7"N 103°51'28.7"E for side road to gate.
GPS: 13°26'27.5"N 103°50'42.5"E.

Like the east gate, the west gate is accessed by a dirt road that leads away from Bayon temple, on the west side of the temple. The road to the gate is also the road that goes past West Prasat Top. Note, the boat picture was taken in Jan 2014, in Dec 2014 on rechecking, the boats were not operational. Service may be started later again.

January 2014.

December 2014.

Angkor Thom

Date: Late 12th century ~ 16th century.
King: Jayavarman VII ~ later rulers.
Religion: Buddhism.
Style: Bayon.
Time: Several hours to two or more days.

Angkor Thom (Large / Great City), is a 10 Km² Khmer City that encompasses several temples, including Bayon and Baphuon Temple. Bayon Temple forms the center of Angkor Thom. The city is surrounded by over 12km of 8m high walls, and has five gates. The walls are built of laterite, and each gate has a 23m high center structure, with a 7m high x 3½m wide entrance, and is richly decorated with faces that resemble King Jayavarman VII, and elephant images (some believe the images may be of Lokeshvara, the Bodhisattva of compassion). The South Gate is normally the first view visitors get to the walls of the city, as they cross over the 100m wide moat that surrounds the city.

The City became the capital, after King Jayavarman VII defeated the Chams, and remained the capital, until the 17th century. Although there were already temples in the city area, such as Baphuon (mid-11th century) and Phimeanakas (10th or early 11th century), King Jayavarman VII built, Bayon Temple to serve as his Royal Palace and State Temple. Due to the Palace being constructed of wood, only the Terraces (Elephant and Leper King Terraces) remain today. Each corner of the city, had a small temple, called Prasat Chrung (Shrine of the Angle). A good example can be seen in the South-West corner of the city that is accessed from the South Gate, by boat or by walking along the inside of the wall. Bicycle tours are run past this temple.

There are a number of footpaths inside the city, where one can explore the forest more if you have time. Interestingly, the road going into the city from the east does not use the East gate, but rather the Victory gate that is offset and not inline with the city center. Both the small and large circuits go through the city, and converge by the Elephant terrace, close to Bayon and Baphuon temple, which are the two largest and most important temples inside the Angkor Thom city, followed by the impressive Elephant terrace.

Bayon Temple

Date: 1181 ~ 1218.
King: Jayavarman VII.
Religion: Buddhism.
Style: Bayon.
Time: 1 to 2 hours.
Best time to visit: Sunrise to early in the morning or late afternoon.
GPS: 13°26'28.3"N 103°51'37.5"E.

Bayon Temple (Golden Tower), is in the center of Angkor Thom, and was King Jayavarman VII's state temple. The temple represents Mount Meru, or the center of the universe in Hindu and Buddhist believe. A 72m long, two-level pathway that is guarded by lions, leads to the eastern gate of the temple. Although the temple was originally built as a Buddhist temple, King Jayavarman VIII converted it to a Hindu temple, and destroyed the Buddhist statues. Interestingly, shrines for both Vishnu and Shiva are found at the temple. The temple is richly decorated with reliefs, with religious and mythological scenes found on the inner galleries and war and daily life scenes found on the outer galleries.

Visitors can easily access the 3rd floor by means of stairs, where sculpted faces, believed to be either of Lokeshvara (the Bodhisattva of compassion) or King Jayavarman VII, as large as 2 ½m are found.

Three enclosures are found at the temple. The ground floor holds the 3rd enclosure, and measures 160m long x 140m wide. Daily life, war scenes, and dancing Apsaras can be found here.

The second enclosure is 80m long x 70m wide. Large faces of Lokeshvara, Hindu religious and mythological scenes, as well as sculptings of Buddha can be found here.

The 1st enclosure consists of the 3rd floor, where Hindu images as well as Buddha faces can be found. The circular central sanctuary is surrounded by eight sanctuary towers with sculpted faces. Four satellite sanctuaries surround them, with the Western sanctuary dedicated to Vishnu, the Northern one to Shiva, and Southern sanctuary to the Buddha.

A 3.6m image of a seated and meditating Buddha, on the coiled body of the snake Mucalinda, was discovered in a pit under the Southern sanctuary. This image is now the Buddha image at Wat Prampei Loveng (see Buddha section). A visit in the early morning or afternoon as the sun sets, gives good views over the Angkor Thom area surrounding the temple, as well as the many large faces on the top floor.

A walkway spans all around the top floor, while being surrounded by large towers with faces in all four directions. The center of the top, contains a large temple structure, with the largest tower in the center.

The faces on the top level are up to 2 ½m high. Believe are that they are of either Lokeshvara (the Bodhisattva of compassion) or King Jayavarman VII. The temple is best visited in the early morning or late afternoon, if you want the sun directly on the faces, and midday to avoid the crowds if you want wide shots of the top area.

South entrance of temple. 12:45Am. Wall with bas-relief on the outside.

December 2014, 7:45Am, only the top tower is bathed in sunlight.

Anton Swanepoel

Outer wall, depicting scenes of battle and daily life.

Anton Swanepoel

Anton Swanepoel

A walkway spans all around the top floor, while being surrounded by large towers with faces in all four directions. The center of the top contains a large temple structure, with the largest tower in the center.

Looking up at the top tower.

Anton Swanepoel

Faces up to 2 ½m high. Believe are that they are of either Lokeshvara (the Bodhisattva of compassion) or King Jayavarman VII. The temple is best visited in the early morning or late afternoon, if you want the sun directly on the faces, and midday to avoid the crowds if you want wide shots of the top area.

Baphuon

Date: 1060.
King: Udayadityavarman II.
Religion: Hindu.
Style: Baphuon.
Time: 1 to 2 hours.
Best time to visit: Anytime for the bas-relief, early in the morning for the East entrance, and sunrise or late afternoon for a view of the surrounding area.
GPS: 13°26'37.5"N 103°51'32.5"E for first terraces.

Baphuon Temple (Tower of Bronze), predates Angkor Thom City, and is surrounded by a 425m x 125m sandstone wall. The temple represents Mount Meru, and is higher than Bayon. The temple was the state temple of Yasodharapura the 11th century.

More than 10 chambers are at its base. Bas-reliefs with daily life and forest scenes, carved in small squares, decorate the temple. The best approach is over a 200m long, elevated walkway on the east side, by the Elephant Terrace.

From the top, one has a superb view of Bayon, Phnom Bakheng in the south and Phimeanakas in the north. The temple has five sandstone bases, with the 1st to 3rd bases surrounded by sandstone galleries. Baphuon is the first style where stone galleries with a central tower are found.
The top level has a central sanctuary with two wings, decorated with animated figures (in restoration), visible from the west side at floor level.

After visiting the temple, turn right as you look at the stairs, then go around to the back and through the wall by an archway, to reach Phimeanakas Temple.

The best entrance is from the Elephant Terrace.

200m walkway, with pools on the sides.

After visiting the temple, turn right as you look at the stairs, then go around to the back and through the wall by an archway, to reach Phimeanakas Temple.

As you enter the grounds, go left, anti-clockwise around.

Anton Swanepoel

Soon you will find two stairways leading up.

The second stairway to the top is steep.

Anton Swanepoel

Looking down at the front, with the causeway to the elephant terrace in the far back.

To get to Phimeanakas, go around, on the left side of the temple. The exit down should take you directly to the back, as you cannot exit where you came up.

As you go around the temple to the back, you will come to a big tree and a rest area. There is an archway in the wall close by.

You can go through the first archway 13°26'40.1"N 103°51'22.3"E, or you can go through the second one by the rest area, next picture.

Second archway through the wall. 13°26'39.5"N 103°51'19.1"E

Anton Swanepoel

Keep following the path to Phimeanakas temple.

Phimeanakas

Date: 950 ~ 1050.
King: Rajendravarman or Suryavarman I.
Religion: Hindu.
Style: Kleang.
Time: ½ hour.
Best time to visit: Early in the morning when the sun shines against the temple front as pictured above.
GPS: 13°26'44.3"N 103°51'22.1"E.

Phimeanakas Temple (Celestial Palace / the Golden Tower), is a laterite, stepped pyramid temple, located near Baphuon, at the center of the Royal Palace enclosure. The temple was used by King Jayavarman VII as his private temple. Two pools next to the temple may have been used for bathing. The remains of an earlier structure, with inscriptions with dedications to Vishnu, dating to 910, were uncovered here. On the door an inscription dated 1011, reads of an oath of allegiance to the Angkor King. The base measures 35m long x 28m wide, and the upper platform 30m long x 23m wide.

The galleries on top of the pyramid were the first vaulted galleries to be built at Angkor. A stele written by King Jayavarman VII's second wife was found in 1916 by Henri Marchal. The stele tells how the king's first and second wife helped spread Buddhism, as well as a number of important events, including the King's coronation in 1181.

Legend foretells that on top of the temple, lived a spirit in the form of a nine headed snake, who is the Lord of the Khmer Kingdom. The spirit took the form of a woman at night, and the King had to climb to the top of the tower and sleep with the spirit. If he failed in his duty, great disaster would befall the Kingdom, and if the spirit did not show, it foretold the Kings death. The temple as with the Royal Pools and terraces, are best visited in the early morning, when the sun bathes them in golden light.

On the mid-section.

Looking up at the top section from the mid-section.

Anton Swanepoel

Looking down at the lower mid-section.

Dedication on top of the temple.

As you walk back to the road towards the Elephant Terraces, you will pass this terrace remains. 13°26'42.6"N 103°51'25.1"E. There are also a number of smaller ruins just past them, and a gate that leads to Baphuon temple.

Royal Palace

Date: Late 12th century ~ early 13th century.

King: Jayavarman VII.

The Royal Palace was situated inside Angkor Thom City, with the palace ground surrounded by a laterite wall. Today, only the base of the palace terrace remains. The grounds were 585m along the N~S axis, and 246m along the E~W axis. A moat surrounded the grounds, with several entrances in the wall.

The Palace grounds contained an entry court to the East, the Royal enclosures with the Royal Palace, an enclosure for women in the West, a number of buildings for the priests, the King's wives and concubines, soldiers, Palace guards and general buildings. As they were all made of wood and other perishable materials, only written accounts of them remain.

The Royal Terraces (Elephant Terrace to the South and the Leper King Terrace to the North) form the eastern boundary of the Royal Palace grounds, and run 400m N ~ S. The terraces face the parade grounds and the Suor Prat towers. It is believed that the parade grounds were used for army parades, games and processions watched by the King from the Terrace of the Elephants. The Royal Pools are situated north of Phimeanakas, and measures 140m. Sculpting of several animals can be seen on the walls.

Gate in the dividing wall between the Royal pools and Phimeanakas temple.

Royal Pools

Date: Late 12th century ~ early 13th century.
King: Jayavarman VII.
Style: Bayon.
Time: ½ hour.
Best time to visit: Early in the morning to catch the reflection of the trees on the water.
GPS: 13°26'48.6"N 103°51'28.2"E.

The Royal Pools are around 200m from Phimeanakas temple, and consist of two large pools in series, that are behind a wall that runs between them and Phimeanakas temple. The pools always contain water, but in the rainy season, the pools are at capacity, and can make for some stunning scenic shots early in the morning or late in the afternoon when the sun hits the pools at an angle.

First pool, the second is directly across from this view. Dec 2014, 7Am.

Second Royal pool. Dec 2014, 7:45Am.

Elephant Terrace

Date: late 12th century.

King: Jayavarman VII.

Religion: Buddhism.

Style: Bayon.

Time: ½ hour.

Best time to visit: Sunrise and early in the morning to catch the light shining directly onto the terrace. Just before midday to get the sun on the hidden relief of a five-headed horse.

GPS: 13°26'49.8"N 103°51'31.8"E.

The Elephant Terrace (Royal Terrace) forms part of the Eastern boundary of the Royal Palace grounds. It is believed that the king watched processions, parades and other events from the Terraces.

The terrace contains extensive sculpting of Devata's, Apsara's, mythological animals and demons and the terrace got its name from the sculptures of elephants found here, where elephant heads protrude out from the wall, with their trunks forming pillars that extend to the ground. (Similar to those of the gates of Angkor Thom.) Chinese diplomat Zhou Daguan that lived in Cambodia for a year, recorded that the king appeared daily on the terrace, to listen to and address complaints and problems of the citizens of his Kingdom.

There is a hidden relief of a five-headed horse at the north end of the terrace.

Anton Swanepoel

Full view of both terraces, starting with the Elephant Terrace, and ending in the Leper Terrace. Baphuon temple is accessed from directly left of this view.

Anton Swanepoel

Anton Swanepoel

Leper King Terrace

Date: late 12th century.
King: Jayavarman VII.
Religion: Buddhism.
Style: Bayon.
Time: ½ hour.
Best time to visit: Sunrise and early in the morning to catch the light shining directly onto the terrace.
GPS: 13°26'50.5"N 103°51'31.7"E.

The Leper King Terrace is 25m long, and directly north of the Elephant Terrace. It is named after the "Leper King" statue that was found here. The statue is believed to be of King Yasovarman I (also known as the Leper King), who suffered from leprosy, although current thought is that the statue might represent Kubera, the god of wealth (also believed to suffer from leprosy), or Yama, the God of death. The original statue is now in Phnom Penh museum, with a copy now decorating the terrace. The terrace is believed to represent Mount Meru, and rows of carved figures of multi headed Naga snakes, armed guardians, Garuda's and female celestial beings, decorate the walls.

Leper King Statue in the distance.

Leper King Statue.

Anton Swanepoel

You can follow a short passage along the decorated wall.

The two terraces runs 400m north – south, with the Elephant terrace the most impressive section. From this view, head directly right, to visit Prasat Preah Palilay and Tep Pranam.

Tep Pranam

Date: End of the 9th century.
King: Yasovarman I.
Religion: Buddhist.
Style: Mixed.
Time: ½ hour.
GPS: 13°26'54.2"N 103°51'29.3"E.

Tep Pranam is 100m north of the Terrace of the Leper King, and is accessed by a dirt path. Although the temple consists of only a few scattered blocks and a 30m laterite causeway as well as a short cross shaped causeway, the surrounding park and other temples, such as Prasat Preah Palilay, makes this a must see. A Buddha statue (assembled from different sandstone blocks), seated on a lotus pedestal, is situated at the end of the walkway. See Tep Pranam Pagoda under Buddha section.

Tep Pranam Pagoda can be seen in the background.

Cross-shaped causeway.

Prasat Preah Palilay

Date: Late 12th or early 13th century.
King: Indravarman II or Jayavarman VIII.
Religion: Buddhist.
Style: Bayon.
Time: ½ hour.
GPS: 13°26'55.5"N 103°51'18.9"E.

Preah Palilay temple is behind the Leper King terrace, past Tep Pranam, and is oriented towards the East. Follow the dirt road that leads into the forest, past Tep Pranam. The Preah Palilay sanctuary is enclosed by a laterite wall, 50m long x 50m wide, with the eastern wall containing a gopura entrance building with a single tower. There is a seated Buddha, a reclining Buddha and several Buddhist stories. One depicts Buddha subduing the elephant Nalagiri, a second depicts where Buddha gives away his two children, and displays the virtue of charity.

Path towards the temple.

Prasat Preah Palilay.

Anton Swanepoel

The Gopura entrance with its single tower, in a section of the wall that surrounds the temple. Although neither the entrance nor the temple are by their own spectacular, their forest setting and quietness makes them good options for a relaxed visit.

Prasat Suor Prat / Prasat Neang 12 / North and South Towers

Date: End of the 13th century.
King: Indravarman II.
Religion: Buddhism.
Style: Post-Bayon.
Time: ½ to 1 hour to see all, or 15 min just to view one.
GPS: 13°26'49.1"N 103°51'36.8"E.

Prasat Suor Prat (towers of the ropedancers), is a row of 12 towers, 6 on either side of the road leading from the Royal Palace to the Victory gate. Large windows are found on three sides, with the sandstone fronts decorated with lions and Naga sculptings. The entrances face towards the parade grounds and terraces. Behind the two towers closest to the road to the Victory gate, is a large pool fitted with laterite steps.

The towers' unusual north – south orientation as to the normal east or west orientation, suggest the towers were not built as sanctuaries, yet their actual use is unknown.

However, theories are that ropes were hung from the top of the towers during festivals, where acrobats then used it to perform acts while the king watched from the Elephant terrace. Zhou Daguan, a Chinese diplomat who resided in Cambodia for a year until 1297, wrote that the towers were used to resolve legal disputes. If two men disagreed, both were locked up in a tower. After four days, the guilty party would have developed some disease. This is called celestial judgment. Another theory suggests that the towers were used as reception halls to receive important guests of the King. The guests would have a view of the parade ground, and be close to the Royal Court.

Mangalartha / East Prasat Top / Monument 487

Date: Late 13th century.
King: Jayavarman VIII.
Religion: Hindu.
Style: Bayon.
Time: 20 min.
GPS: 13°26'44.8"N 103°52'06.0"E for side road.
GPS: 13°26'36.4"N 103°52'05.2"E for temple.

Mangalartha, is the last known temple in the Angkor period, and is 500m west of the Victory Gate, and 286m into the forest. The temple is made of sandstone, and was built in honor of a Brahman scholar called Jayamangalartha, who was the son of one of the gurus of Jayavarman VIII. Jayamangalartha is said to have reached 104 years of age. This is a little gem of a temple and with the forest setting and secludedness, makes for a nice visit.

Path to the temple, December 2014.

North and South Khleang / Storehouses

Date: Late 10th century to early 11th century.
King: Jayavarman (North), Suryavarman I (South).
Style: Khleang.
Time: ½ hour.
GPS: 13°26'49.7"N 103°51'38.6"E (North Khleang).
GPS: 13°26'40.3"N 103°51'38.8"E (South Khleang).

These structures are opposite the Elephant and Leaper Terraces, and behind the North and South towers of the Preah Pithu group. The north building measures 40m x 4.7m, with 1.5m thick walls. The south building is the same length, but only 4.2m wide, and was built at a later date. The south building is not to the same standard as the north, as well as being incomplete. It is believed that the builder of the south tower may have been rushed, as it lacks in workmanship and detail when compared to the north tower.

This is the South Khleang, behind the Southernmost Prasat Sour Prat tower, across from the Elephant Terrace.

Date: 12th century.
King: Jayavarman VII.
Style: Bayon.
Time: 10 min at temple, getting there about 30 min.
GPS: 13°25'33.2"N 103°51'24.7"E.

Prasat Chrung (Shrine of the Angle / The corner Shrine), is one of four temples built in the Angkor Thom City walls, one at each corner. This one is in a good state. To reach the temple, you have to either take a boat ride from the south gate, or walk along the inside of the wall to it. The temples contain a stele that praises King Jayavarman VII. The temples were dedicated to Bodhisattva Lokeshvara.

South-West Prasat Chrung.

This is the best-preserved one at the moment, and a popular stop for bicycle tours. If you take a boat ride from the south gate, the boat will stop at a dock a short distance away from the temple, where you can use wooden steps to gain access to the temple.

Preah Pithu Group

Date: First half of the 12th century, 13th century.
King: Suryavarman II, Jayavarman VIII.
Religion: Four are Hindu (dedicated to Shiva), the largest is Buddhist.
Style: Angkor Wat to post-Bayon.
Time: ½ to 1 hour.
GPS: 13°26'55.6"N 103°51'35.2"E (start of temples).

Preah Pithu Group, consist of 5 temples, situated to the North East of the Royal Palace, behind the Prasat Sour Prat towers, and start directly behind the Khmer restaurants and end by two elephant statues. The temples are surrounded by a beautiful forest landscape that is worth the visit in itself. No steles were found, thus the actual names of these temples are not known. The temples have been named Preah Pithu T, to Preah Pithu Y, skipping W. Note, as there are no signs for the temples; names are placed to the closest temple shown on google maps to the GPS coordinates for the structure.

The largest temple was not completed. It is thought that the group is an extension of the Leaper King terrace.

Start of the group, near the restrooms and Khmer restaurants.

Preah Pithu T. 13°26'54.0"N 103°51'36.4"E.

Preah Pithu U. 13°26'53.9"N 103°51'40.0"E.

Anton Swanepoel

Preah Pithu X. 13°26'54.6"N 103°51'43.0"E.

Preah Pithu V 13°26'56.4"N 103°51'40.5"E.

West Prasat Top / Monument 486

Date: 9th ~ 17th century.
Religion: Theravada Buddhism.
Style: Mixed.
Time: 15 minutes.
GPS: 13°26'22.6"N 103°51'07.2"E.

West Prasat Top is a short distance down Carpeaux road, and 1km from Bayon temple. The road leading off to the temple is the same road that goes to the West gate. The temple is one of the oldest temples in the Angkor Thom City. West Prasat top is a single sanctuary on a laterite platform that is believed to be from the 10th century, although a 9th century inscription was discovered here, and could be from an earlier temple. The temple changed over time, beginning with the transformation to Buddhism around the 13th century, and going up to the 17th century. At this time, the laterite platform was refaced with sandstone, and the sanctuary decorated with pink sandstone lintels and columns. Two additional towers were also erected.

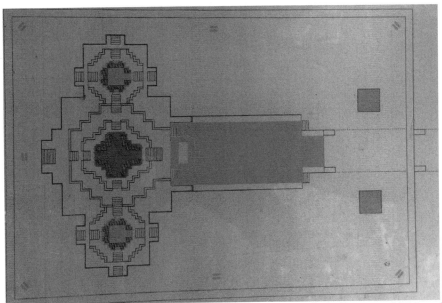

Layout of the temple when restored. I viewed the temple in January 2014 and then again in December 2014, and restoration was still ongoing.

Vong Toch / Small Circuit

The small circuit starts at the T-junction right by the road that leads around Angkor Wat, and is 5km from national road 6 in town on the road that passes the ticket office. The small circuit road continues for 5.6km, where a T-junction is found by Srah Srang. The small circuit turns left and continues through Angkor Thom City, past Bayon and Angkor Wat temples, to loop back to the start point. At the T-junction at Srah Srang, if you turn right, you would follow the Grand circuit. Total distance of the small circuit is 17.3km with a loop from and to town making 27.3km.

In this book, temples included in the small circuit include all the temples from Angkor Wat temple, past the split between the small and grand circuit, up to the Victory gate. The temples between the South Gate and Angkor Wat temple, are listed under their own section. Although the route goes through Angkor Thom City, these temples along the road are listed under the Angkor Thom City section.

Angkor Wat

Date: First half of the 12th century.
King: Suryavarman II.
Religion: Hindu.
Style: Angkor Wat.
Time: Minimum 1 day, (suggests two half days, morning and afternoon).
Best time to visit: Early in the morning to catch the sun rising over Angkor, and late afternoon to get good pictures of the sun from behind you. To avoid the crowds, come at midday when everyone else is eating.
GPS: 13°24'45.2"N 103°51'34.1"E.

Angkor Wat (temple city) is 1.6km from the south gate of Angkor Thom City (main entrance), and is the most impressive temple in the park. The temple features on the national flag, and is a major pull for tourists to Cambodia. A 190m wide moat surrounds the complex that span an impressive 1.5km long x 1.3 km wide.

The temple is unlike other Angkor temples in orientation, facing west and dedicated to Vishnu, where other temples face east and are dedicated to Shiva. Some believe the west facing was that the temple served as a funerary temple, as the setting sun symbolizes the end of the cycle of life. Angkor Wat is believed to represent Mount Meru, the center of the world in Hindu cosmology, with the temple's five sanctuary towers representing the peaks of the sacred mountain, while the moat represents the ocean that surrounds Mount Meru. Intricate bas reliefs that depict scenes from epic Ramayana and Mahabharata battles and events, as well as statues of female devas, draw visitors to the temple.

The main entrance is on the western end by means of a 12m wide x 190m long bridge, where lions and Naga snakes guard the temple.

The temple took only 35 years to build, and is an architectural wonder. The temple is in fact floating on an artificial island, with the massive surrounding moat, providing water to keep the temple floated in the dry season. This ingenious setup, allows the complex to be at ground level, without the need to be built on a mountain as other large temples, while not being affected by the shifting ground as it expands and contracts in the wet and dry season respectively.

A 12m wide bridge span over the 190m wide moat.

After the gate, is a 350m processional causeway, elevated about 1½ meters, flanked by a library building on either side, followed by two pools.

Jan 2014.

Workers cleaning the moat. December 2014.

December 2014, moat full, and water clear. In the early morning, the sun comes up over Angkor, and is good for a view, but bad for pictures if you want to capture the iconic front, in the afternoon the sun sets behind this view and allows for excellent pictures of Angkor Wat's iconic front. Suggest to do two half days here, one morning with a sunrise; and one afternoon with a sunset.

350m long causeway. The buildings on either side are libraries.

Library building, the North Angkor pagoda is to the far left, as well as the toilets, roadside Khmer restaurants, and an information office.

View of the front courtyard, from the temple towards the entrance.

Libraries and causeway running between them to the temple.

Anton Swanepoel

The temple platform is 330m long x 255m wide.

Decorated ceiling tiles.

Bakan

Originally, the principal sanctuary of Angkor Vat's uppermost terrace, called "Bakan", was open to the four cardinal points, and probably sheltered a statue of Vishnu. Later, when Angkor Vat became a center of Buddhist pilgrimage, the four entranceways into the central sanctuary were filled in with sandstone; each of the newly constituted walls was then sculpted with a relief of the standing Buddha. 20th-century investigations inside the sanctuary revealed multiple statue and pedestal fragments, of which two pieces are of particular note: a statue of the Buddha seated on a naga, which is now venerated in Bakan's eastern gallery, and a rectangular stone object thought to have served as a sarcophagus. A number of such objects, in which the corpse would have been placed in a foetal position, have been found in other Angkorian temples.

APSARA

A 50m bas-relief showing the turning of the sea event. In total, there are some 600m of bas-relief and nearly 2000 apsaras.

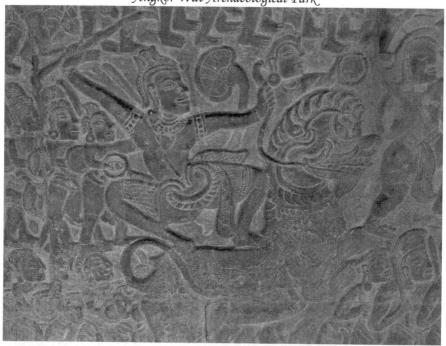

Anton Swanepoel

Anton Swanepoel

Buddha in central tower.

Looking up at one of the corners of the central sanctuary.

Anton Swanepoel

A 42m high central sanctuary, with Buddha statues, is situated in the middle of the Angkor Wat complex. Note, no hats or anything that covers your head are allowed (must be removed), and no open shoulders or pants and dresses that do not cover the knees. Tripods and video cameras are also not allowed.

Inside the central sanctuary.

Anton Swanepoel

Looking over the courtyard to the front gate of Angkor.

Central tower on the top section of Angkor Wat Temple.

Saying goodbye to Angkor Wat temple is always difficult.

Anton Swanepoel

Angkor Wat Side entrance

Date: First half of the 12th century.
King: Suryavarman II.
Religion: Hindu.
Style: Angkor Wat.
Time: 10 minutes.
GPS: 13°24'44.8"N 103°52'25.1"E.

This is a gateway to the back entrance to Angkor Wat temple, and offers a very nice walk along a dirt path, flanked by forests. From the start of either the small or the grand circuit, at the T-junction with the road that runs along the Angkor Wat moat and the road from town, turn right and follow the road for 1.2km. Take the side road on the left just before you go over a bridge. If you go with a tuk tuk, you can either have him wait here, or pick you up at the main entrance of Angkor Wat temple if you feel like walking all the way through.

Angkor Wat calls in the distance.

Offerings are done at the gate, as many other places. Do know that if you take an incense stick, you are expected to give a donation to the monk or nun. The same goes with any armbands that they give you, if you do not want to give a donation, do not take any offerings.

Prasat Kravan

Date: 921.
King: High-ranking priest of King Harshavarman I.
Religion: Hindu.
Style: Bakheng to Koh Ker.
Time: 20 ~ 30 minutes.
Best time to visit: Sunrise for the towers, morning to midday for the bas-reliefs.
GPS: 13°25'10.7"N 103°53'58.0"E.

Prasat Kravan (the cardamom sanctuary) is a 5-stupa sanctuary, 3km from the back entrance to Angkor Wat Temple, and was dedicated to Vishnu, the Supreme God of Hinduism. The sculptures found inlaid directly in the brickwork of the towers, are unique in Angkor, and more found in Cham temples in Vietnam.

This is the only temple in Angkor that features artwork that stands out of the brickwork. An extensive restoration has been completed, with minor restoration ongoing.

This is the only temple in Angkor that features artwork that stands out of the brickwork. An extensive restoration has been completed, with minor restoration ongoing.

Prasat Bat Chum

Date: Mid-10th century.
King: Buddhist Minister Kavindra-rimathana during King Rajendravarman's reign.
Religion: Buddhism.
Style: Pre Rup.
Time: 15 minutes.
GPS: 13°25'29.5"N 103°54'29.2"E.

Prasat Bat Chum is a three tower, temple that according to an inscription dated 953 AD, the temple was built by architect Kavindrarimathana (the only Khmer architect whose name is known), who also built King Rajendravarman's Royal palace, East Mebon and Srah Srang.

From Prasat Kravan, go 600m along the road, then turn right into road 661 at 13°25'25.0"N 103°54'05.1"E. Go 900m down road 661, then turn left into a side road at 13°25'20.6"N 103°54'33.2"E. Follow this road to the temple.

Banteay Kdei

Date: Late 12th century – early 13th.
King: Jayavarman II, enhanced by Indravarman II.
Religion: Buddhism.
Style: Angkor Wat and Bayon.
Time: ½ hour.
GPS: 13°25'47.3"N 103°53'42.1"E. First entrance.
GPS: 13°25'48.5"N 103°54'07.2"E. Second entrance that is opposite Srah Srang, and offers a nice view of Srah Srang.

Banteay Kdei (citadel of the cells), is directly opposite Srah Srang, and 4.2km from the Victory gate, outside Angkor Thom City. The temple was built of soft sandstone, with the outer wall enclosing the temple, built with reused laterite stones, and measures 700m x 500m. The innermost enclosure measures 320m x 300m. Much of the temple is in ruin, and lends to the appeal of the temple, coupled with the jungle setting. The temple is believed to have been built over an existing temple, dating from the 10th century. Banteay Kdei itself is believed to have been used as a Buddhist monastery.

A good time to visit is early in the morning, or late in the afternoon.

274 Buddha statues were found here in 2001.

Anton Swanepoel

Ask your tuk tuk driver to meet you at the second entrance, and then walk through the complex to see its entire splendor.

Srah Srang / Royal Bathing Pool

Date: 10th century, with alteration in late 12th century.
King: Rajendravarman, alterations by Jayavarman VII.
Style: Bayon.
Time: 15 minutes to ½ hour.
GPS: 13°25'48.7"N 103°54'08.5"E.

Srah Srang (Royal bathing Srah / pool) is a 700m long x 350m wide water reservoir, across from Banteay Kdei temple. Khmer restaurants are situated here and makes for a good rest stop. About 5 to 10 minutes. Just a walkover from Banteay Kdei's suggested entrance.

The Srah was used as a common bathing Srah, and for ritual events. A 10th century inscription found nearby, urged the people not to bathe animals in the Srah, nor let herds of elephants destroy the Srah. King Jayavarman VII added laterite stone steps to aid in access to the Srah. There was an artificial island with a sanctuary in the middle of the Srah. Sunrise (from the embarkation terrace across Banteay Kdei) and sunset (from the East side of the Srah) with a reflection of the sun on the waters can be seen from here.

It is believed that boats were launched from here to take the king around the Srah.

Anton Swanepoel

Khmer habitat interpretation center

Time: 20 minutes.
GPS: 13°25'56.7"N 103°54'04.7"E.

The Khmer Habitat center is just after Banteay Kdei and Srah Srang, down the road that leads to Kutisvara and Ta Prohm Temple.

The site has a Khmer house, small garden, farm implements, and is to show visitors how Khmers in the countryside live. Entrance is free, and a guide is situated at the house.

Anton Swanepoel

Kutisvara

Date: 9th century.
King: Jayavarman II.
Religion: Hindu.
Style: Pre Rup, Preah Ko for central tower.
Time: 15 minutes.
GPS: 13°25'56.5"N 103°53'59.4"E. Side road to take from main road.
GPS: 13°26'02.6"N 103°53'59.3"E.

Originally a small brick temple with three towers, now in ruin, but with the forest setting and historical interest, still worth a visit. The temple is 200m from the main road, down a dirt path and through some rice fields. From the road that passes Srah Srang, turn left at the T-junction, and go 250m down the road as going to Ta Prohm, look for a small side road into the forest on your right. Go 200m down this road. The temple itself is in Kutisvara Oxcart community, so you can walk around and see how the locals live and maybe hop on a traditional oxcart as it passes you if you ask the owner nicely.

This is how the road looked in Dec 2014. The temple is on the small hill, by the big tree in the back that is slightly to the right of the road.

Ta Prohm

Date: Late 12th century – early 13th century.
King: Jayavarman VII.
Religion: Buddhism.
Style: Bayon.
Time: 1 to 3 hours.
Best time to visit: Early in the morning to avoid the crowds, or late afternoon when everyone heads to Phnom Bakheng.
GPS: 13°26'05.3"N 103°53'06.6"E. Suggested entrance.

Ta Prohm is outside the SW corner of the East baray, and 2.5km from the Victory Gate of Angkor Thom City. The temple was dedicated to Prajnaparamita, King Jayavarman VII's mother, and is now known as the 'Angelina Jolie Temple' that featured in the movie, Tomb Raider, where Angelina played Lara Croft. This fame from the movie, coupled with the attractive jungle setting, makes it one of the most visited temples in the park.

A stele, dated 1186, and written in ancient Sanskrit language, was found here, and was a treasure trove of information about products used for religious ceremonies, the mention of the 102 hospital chapels, the number of priests and people living at Ta Prohm, as well as mention of 121 rest houses across the empire that spread as far away as Phimai in Thailand and the Kingdom of Champa in present day Vietnam. From inscriptions, it was noted that over 80 thousand people maintained this complex (villagers and lay people).

As with many other temples, a large moat surrounds the temple, and access is by bridges and walkways.

The temple has two entrances, with the one facing Angkor Thom City normally used as starting point. Tuk tuk drivers normally drop you off at one entrance, and pick you up at the other. There are more than just one tree growing over the walls of the temple, however, if you want to get a picture without 20 thousand other visitors in the shot, then either go early in the morning (around 7 to 8am, or late in the afternoon, around 4pm).

Anton Swanepoel

This is the backside of a tree pictured featured next.

The front side of the pictured noted before that showed the back of the tree and the wall.

Anton Swanepoel

The snake tree.

Anton Swanepoel

The famous tree that featured in the movie Tomb Raider.

Anton Swanepoel

Time: 10 minutes.
GPS: 13°26'34.3"N 103°53'06.2"E for side road.
GPS: 13°26'34.5"N 103°53'09.4"E for temple.

West Prasat Top2 (as per google maps) is 100m into the forest, by a side road on the right, 900m past Ta Prohm's west gate.

Chapel of the hospital

Date: Late 12th century.
King: Jayavarman VII.
Religion: Buddhism.
Style: Bayon.
Time: 15 min.
GPS: 13°26'43.1"N 103°52'50.6"E.
GPS: 13°26'45.3"N 103°52'50.0"E, side entrance with rest area.

The chapel of the hospital is on the left of the corner of the road between Ta Keo, and Spean Thma temple. An inscription found in the area confirms this temple as one of the 102 arogayasals (chapel hospitals) found throughout the empire. Four were built by King Jayavarman VII, around Angkor Thom City. The floor plan is in the shape of a cross, and has an east-facing door. The exterior is adorned by female divinities, with images of Buddha also found.

Anton Swanepoel

Date: 975 – around 1000.
King: Jayavarman V, Jayaviravarman.
Religion: Hindu.
Style: Khleang.
Time: 1 hour.
GPS: 13°26'38.1"N 103°52'56.6"E.

Ta Keo temple (originally Hema-sringagiri, meaning 'The mountain with the golden peaks'), is 1.3 km from the Victory gate, outside Angkor Thom City, just past the Chapel of the hospital. The temple is a sandstone mountain temple, dedicated to Shiva, and the tallest monument of Angkor. The temple has five sanctuaries on top of a 22m high, five stepped pyramid, and served as the state temple for Jayavarman V. The temple was never completed, and an inscription reads that lightning struck the temple and was taken as a sign of bad luck upon which work was halted. Whether that is the reason why work stopped, is unknown.

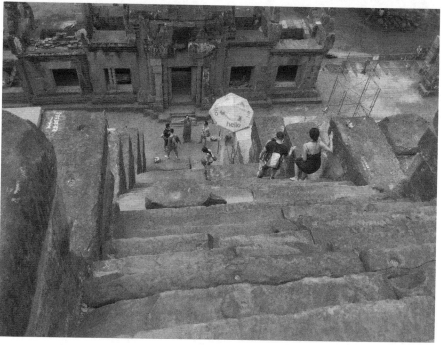

Anton Swanepoel

Date: 16th century.
Style: Post Bayon.
Time: 10 minutes.
GPS: 13°26'46.0"N 103°52'47.3"E.

Spean Thma (the stone bridge) is just after the chapel of the hospital, and after a bridge. The structure was a bridge, constructed of reused blocks of sandstone, and thought to have replaced an earlier bridge. The interesting thing to note is that the bride now follows the path of the river, suggesting that the direction of the river might have changed.

The ruins are a favorite place for local kids to play, while parents have picnics on the riverbank and the grass area behind the bridge.

Chao Say Tevoda

Date: End 11th century – early 12th century.
King: Suryavarman II, Yasovarman II, Jayavarman.
Religion: Hindu.
Style: Angkor Wat.
Time: ½ hour.
Best time to visit: Early to mid-morning.
GPS: 13°26'43.8"N 103°52'40.2"E.

Chao Say Tevoda is 500m from the Victory Gate, outside Angkor Thom City, and directly across from Thommanon. These two temples are often confused as being planned together, but Chao Say Tevoda was built later than Thommanon. They were also not planned to line up with the Victory lane (road leading to the Royal Palace), as this was built later.

Thommanon

Date: Early 12th century.
King: Suryavarman II.
Religion: Hindu.
Style: Angkor Wat.
Time: ½ hour.
Best time to visit: Early to mid-morning.
GPS: 13°26'48.6"N 103°52'39.4"E.

Thommanon is 500m from the Victory Gate, outside Angkor Thom City, and directly across from Chao Say Tevoda. As mentioned under Chao Say Tevoda, the temples were not built at the same time.

Thommanon temple is the purest Angkorian style dedicated to Brahmanism. It is believed the temple was built at the time when work on Angkor Wat was started.

The temple may have served as a test for the Angkor style.

Ta Nei

Date: Late 12th century.
King: Jayavarman VII, Indravarman II.
Religion: Buddhism.
Style: Bayon.
Time: 45 minutes to 1 ½, Travel time and seeing garden nearby.
GPS: 13°27'09.1"N 103°53'07.7"E.

Ta Nei is 1.1km down a dirt road that starts about 130m from the back entrance to the Ta Keo temple. The dirt road makes an S just after the start, keep left (flight of the gibbon is on the same road). Continue on this road for about 1km to Approx. 13°27'08.4"N 103°52'60.0"E, where you will find a sign and a side road that leads to the temple. The road leading to the temple is scenic, and a nice cycle route. There is also a picnic area, (botanical garden according to the sign) situated nearby the temple.

The initial complex was 35m x 26m, however; King Rajendravarman enlarged it to 55m x 47m.

Time: 30 minutes.
GPS: 13°27'18.8"N 103°53'09.8"E.

The botanical garden, seem from the signpost to indicate a rest area, a short distance from Ta Nei temple, and across a bridge. Locals love to use this place as picnic, for the scenery and seclusion. Follow the Road to Ta Nei temple, and keep going directly past it, into the forest. The path will change to a channel that runs along the river, and end by the bride. You can easily cross the bridge, to get to the picnic spot on the other side.

Time to go back, keep the balance.

Rest area across the bridge.

Vong Thom / Grand Circuit

As with the small circuit, the grand circuit starts at the T-junction right
by the road that leads around the Angkor Wat temple, and is 5km
from national road 6 in town on the road that passes the ticket office.
The grand circuit road continues for 5.6km, where a T-junction is
found by Srah Srang. The grand circuit turns right, and continues
through the East Baray, past Ta Som, Neak Pean, and Preah Khan,
then through the North gate and passes by the Leper and Elephant
terraces, Bayon, and on to pass by Angkor Wat Temple. Total distance
of the grand circuit is 25.2km with a loop from and to town 35.2km.

In this book, temples listed under the grand circuit, are temples found
after the split in the road between the small and grand circuit, by Srah
Srang, and up to the North gate of Angkor Thom City.

Date: 961.
King: Rajendravarman.
Religion: Hindu.
Style: Banteay Srei.
Time: ½ hour to 1 hour.
Best time to visit: Sunrise to early morning, and late afternoon to sunset.
GPS: 13°26'06.0"N 103°55'17.2"E.

The Pre Rup (change the body/ enlightenment) was the state temple of King Rajendravarman. The temple is 7.9km from the start of the grand circuit, and has several towers, with the central tower containing a sanctuary room. The lintels contain Indra riding the elephant Airavata, Vishnu on Garuda (a large mythological bird, the mount of Vishnu), and other scenes. The temple complex is 127m x 117m large.

Anton Swanepoel

Prasat Leak Neang

Time: 10 minutes.
GPS: 13°26'08.9"N 103°55'17.6"E. Side of the main road to start.
GPS: 13°26'09.8"N 103°55'20.5"E. Temple.

Prasat Leak Neang, is a single structure stupa, around 95m from the road into the forest, 115m from the east entrance of Pre Rup, and around 35m from a side road going off to the right.

View from the road in Dec 2014. The temple is right by the tall tree seen in the background. A part of the temple is visible just to the right of the tree. Note, the cow may have moved when you get there. ☺

East Baray

Date: 889.
King: Yasovarman I.
Time: 5 minutes.
GPS: 13°26'21.5"N 103°55'17.1"E to 13°27'20.9"N 103°54'42.6"E.

The East Baray, originally Yasodharatataka, meaning 'reservoir of Yasodhara', is a water reservoir, measuring 7.5 km x 1.83 km and could hold 55 million cubic meters of water, with the depth being 4m, but is mostly dry today. You can stop at points along the grand circuit as it cuts through the baray, to take in the countryside.

East Mebon

Date: 953.
King: Rajendravarman.
Religion: Hindu
Style: Pre Rup.
Time: 1 hour.
Best time to visit: Sunrise to early morning, or late afternoon to sunset.
GPS: 13°26'47.8"N 103°55'15.2"E.

East Mebon sits atop a fabricated island, and is not a mountain temple. The confusion comes from the appearance of height, due to the baray being dry. Water would have come up around 5m, around the temple. The temple itself has a laterite base of 126m x 121m, and has five towers on the top level, with a library on each corner of the lower level, with galleries on the first level. Elephant statues stand guard on each corner.

Anton Swanepoel

Time: 10 minutes.
GPS: 13°27'12.6"N 103°54'49.1"E.

Oisca Forest Park, is a park, 1.3km from Prasat Ta Som, in the east Baray, and consists of a park where 87 members of Oisca Shikoku, planted 21000 trees during 2005 and 2009.

Anton Swanepoel

Prasat Ta Som

Date: Late 12th century.
King: Jayavarman VII, enlarged by Indravarman II.
Religion: Buddhism.
Style: Bayon (3rd period).
Time: ½ hour.
Best time to visit: Early morning or late afternoon.
GPS: 13°27'52.1"N 103°54'42.9"E.

Prasat Ta Som is 7km from the North Gate, and a small temple complex of 240m x 200m wide, and is most famous for the tree growing over the back entrance. Ta Som was dedicated to King Jayavarman's ancestors. Both the East and West gopura entrances of the laterite outer enclosure have large faces of Lokeshvara, the Bodhisattva of compassion, that face in all four directions. The temple itself is oriented towards the East, and has three enclosures and a moat surrounding a single sanctuary tower in the center of the temple. Although dedicated to Buddha, the lintels and pediments contain sculpting of Hindu depictions that was added later. To get to the famous tree over the entrance, walk directly through the entire complex to the back.

West Entrance used to access the temple.

Anton Swanepoel

Anton Swanepoel

Backside of the entrance with the tree.

This is the famous tree of Ta Som that grows over the entrance. It can get busy here, so come either early in the morning or late in the afternoon if you want to get a picture without 20 people in the shot, or without waiting ½ hour to get a picture.

Krol Ko

Date: 12th ~ early 13th century.
King: Jayavarman VII.
Religion: Buddhism.
Style: Bayon.
Time: 10 minutes.
GPS: 13°28'03.1"N 103°53'46.1"E. Side road.
GPS: 13°28'06.1"N 103°53'44.6"E. Temple.

Prasat Krol Ko (the cattle shed) is a rustic monument, 100m down a dirt path, about 100m from the road leading to the entrance to Neak Pean. Parts of the outer wall still stand, and a number of small structures. There is a small, now dry, baray next to the temple.

Anton Swanepoel

Neak Pean

Date: Second half of the 12th century.
King: Jayavarman VII.
Religion: First Hindu, then later Buddhism.
Style: Bayon.
Time: ½ to 1 hour.
Best time to visit: Early in the morning or late afternoon, with the wet season the best time of year. Mid-November to Mid-January.
GPS: 13°28'02.5"N 103°53'41.3"E (start of walkway).

Neak Pean (the entwined snakes/ serpents) is a temple situated on an island in the center of Jayatataka baray, a 3,5km long x 900m wide water reservoir. The square temple complex is surrounded by 350m laterite walls, and is reached by a raised, 400m long wooden walkway. Initially a royal Hindu site, then rededicated to Buddha with the addition of the four gargoyles, then later rededicated to Lokeshvara, the Bodhisattva of compassion (believed to possess the powers of healing). Only the central pond and four surrounding ponds remain, and are laid out in the shape of a lotus flower.

The central pond measure 70m x 70m, and symbolizes Lake Anavatapta, a lake located in the center of the world in Buddhist cosmology. The smaller ponds (srah), measure 20m x 20m, and have chapels that link the ponds to the main pond. Each chapel is decorated by a different stone gargoyle in a shape, and are the head of an ox, a lion, an elephant, and a horse. Water flowed down from the central pond, through the gargoyles' open mouths into their corresponding chapel's basins. The water flowing down into the small ponds, symbolize the lake meadows of the Kailash Mountain in the Tibet. The ponds were used by pilgrims to wash away their sins.

The central pond has a 14m in diameter stone island that is encircled by two Naga snakes that guard the East and West entrances. The West Nagas' tales are intertwined, and gives the name of the temple complex. Initially, it was Rajyasri (the fortune of the kingdom), as written on a stele at Preah Khan temple. Several lingas of Shiva and Yonis are found around the central sanctuary, and Balaha (a flying horse), is situated by the east entrance. Balaha is said to rescue stranded merchants from the island Singhala, that is inhabited by demons in the form of young women.

During the wet season, most of the area is flooded. Jan 2014.

Even in the dry season, the walkway is surrounded by water. Jan 2014.

Anton Swanepoel

The green is floating plants, not grass. December 2014.

December 2014. Baray full, and dead trees removed.

Main pond with central structure. Jan 2014. Nagas are dry.

December 2014. Pond filled and Nagas mostly underwater.

Anton Swanepoel

A side pond, with its small chapel. Jan 2014.

December 2014. Pond filled.

Small chapel linking the side pond to the central one. Jan 2014.

December 2014.

Anton Swanepoel

Flying horse and lingas, in the central pond. Jan 2014.

December 2014. The Nagas are almost underwater, as well as the second statue behind the horse. At current, it is not possible to walk around the central pond.

Prasat Prei

Date: 12th century.
King: Jayavarman VII.
Religion: Buddhism.
Style: Bayon.
Time: 10 minutes.
GPS: 13°28'01.2"N 103°52'38.5"E for turn off.
GPS: 13°28'04.4"N 103°52'39.3"E for Temple.

Prasat Prei (the forest sanctuary) is 3.1km from the north gate, down a small dirt road that leads down from the restroom at the corner, and is the first of two structures on this road, with Banteay Prei being second. The central tower has been restored, but from the road the collapsed outer wall (at time of writing), makes it look not worth a visit, which it is. A visit to here should include Banteay Prei next door.

Restored central tower.

Banteay Prei

Date: Late 12th century.
King: Jayavarman VII.
Religion: Buddhism.
Style: Bayon.
Time: ½ hour.
GPS: 13°28'01.2"N 103°52'38.5"E for turn off.
GPS: 13°28'09.7"N 103°52'37.5"E for temple.

Banteay Prei (the forest citadel) is 3.4km from the North gate, and the second temple complex on the dirt road leading from the grand circuit road. The temple is a short distance from Prasat Prei. Much of the temple complex has been restored, however, with the forest surroundings, the partially collapsed sections, and being less visited, this complex makes a good spot to sit and relax for a while. If you are on a bicycle, this is a good spot, as restrooms are a short distance away. The outer moat at times is filled with water, and lends to the splendor of the complex.

The footpath leading to the temple goes through scenic areas.

The inner wall of the complex, after passing by the collapsed outer wall.
August 2014, dry.

December 2014.

Inner complex.

Inner complex.

This is the back entrance of the complex.

Anton Swanepoel

Preah Khan / Kompong Svay

Date: 1191 (for city, original complex early 11th century).
King: Jayavarman VII, with alterations by Jayavarman VIII.
Religion: Buddhism later changed to Hindu.
Style: Bayon.
Time: 1 to 3 hours.
Best time to visit: Anytime for the complex, with late afternoon being best for the NE building pictured above.
GPS: 13°28'01.5"N 103°52'40.6"E.

Preah Khan, (City of the Sacred Sword), is located just outside Angkor Thom City, approximately 2km after the Northern Gate, and was a small city itself, as well as a Buddhist university. From a stele it is known that close to 100,000 people were dedicated to serve this complex. It is thought that the complex may have been the palace of Yasovarman II and Tribhuvanadityavarman.
References indicate that a major battle against the Chams occurred here when Angkor was retaken, and that the Cham king may have died here. Preah Khan was dedicated to Dharanindravarman, Jayavarman VII's father. A moat, measuring 800m x 700m, surrounds the complex, and gives some of the best water views when approaching the temple.
There are three entrances in use, and I recommend the one directly off Banteay Prei and Prasat Prei, where the toilets are. There are a great number of buildings to see here, as well as trees growing over the walls and structures, in the same manner as Ta Prohm.

Many of the Buddhist figures had been destroyed and replaced by Hindu figures by King Jayavarman VIII in the 13th century.

Observation deck, before you get to the temple.

Pathway to the temple.

View from the bridge, of the moat going around the temple.

As you enter, you will pass a small temple building.

Anton Swanepoel

This is my favorite entrance; note the tree on the left growing over the temple.

Tree as noted from the picture before.

Krol Romeas / Krol Damrei

King: Jayavarman VII.
Religion: Buddhism.
Time: 15 minutes.
GPS: 13°27'31.9"N 103°51'47.4"E for road.
GPS: 13°27'29.9"N 103°51'47.5"E for temple.

Krol Romeas is 700m from the North Gate, and about 50m down a dirt path into the forest. The complex was only discovered in 1924, and thought to have been a holding area for elephants. The path leading down is just before the second right bend on the road as you come from the North Gate. Only a 70m diameter circular outer wall of the complex remains. However, the walk in the forest makes for a relaxed visit

Path as you walk to the temple.

Prasat Tonle Snguot

Time: 10 minutes.
GPS: 13°27'23.8"N 103°51'32.9"E for first road.
GPS: 13°27'35.2"N 103°51'33.0"E for second road.
GPS: 13°27'35.1"N 103°51'31.1"E for temple.

Prasat Tonle Snguot is 600m from the North gate. Take the dirt road 200m from the gate, travel about 350m down the dirt road, then turn left into a small footpath, the temple is about 80m down the path. Only a central tower remains of the structure, but the forest setting and the closeness to the North Gate makes this a quick and rewarding visit.

This is a secluded spot, and one can rest here while listing to birds if on a cycle tour. Not many people come here, as the temple is not a main attraction for either history or its looks. If you come by tuk tuk, then you will have to walk most of the way, as the path is narrow.

Temples between Angkor Wat Temple and Angkor Thom City

The following temples are situated between the Angkor Thom City, and Angkor Wat Temple complex. They are on the route for both the small and grand circuit. They are in order, as you will find them when coming from Angkor Wat Temple complex, as most visitors will be taken from Angkor Wat Temple, to Bayon, Baphuon, and the terraces.

Ta Prohm Kel

Date: 1186.
King: Jayavarman VII.
Religion: Buddhism.
Style: Bayon.
Time: 10 minutes.
GPS: 13°24'55.0"N 103°51'32.0"E.

Ta Prohm Kel is 350m from the main Angkor Wat Temple gateway, down a small road that leads off to the left. Currently, only a single tower remains of the sandstone temple, with its opening facing east. This is another of the 102 hospital chapels built around the area. A legend goes that a paralyzed beggar was cured here, and flew away with the horse of Indra.

Prasat Rorng Ramong

Time: 10 minutes.
GPS: 13°25'19.5"N 103°51'35.2"E.

This temple structure consists of a single stupa, situated 26m into the forest, on a dirt road, 1.1km from the main Angkor Wat causeway.

Anton Swanepoel

Phnom Bakheng

Date: Dedicated around 907.
King: Yasovarman I.
Religion: Hindu.
Style: Bakheng.
Time: 1 to 3 hours (including climbing up).
Best time to visit: Sunrise and early in the morning give good views with normally few people around. Midday gives good photo opportunity of the surrounding landscape. Late afternoon and sunset is worth it, however, at sunset time it can get very crowded here.
GPS: 13°25'25.8"N 103°51'34.4"E.

Phnom Bakheng (originally Yasodharapura) is a mountain temple dedicated to Shiva, and located on mountain Bakheng, 400m before the South Gate.

The temple was the state temple of the first city at Angkor. King Yasovarman I, moved the capital from, now Roluos group (Hariharalaya), to here, until 928, when it was abandoned until 968, when King Jayavarman V briefly used it.

The entire hill was surrounded by a moat measuring 650m x 436m, of which parts of it is still visible. In total, there were 108 smaller towers, with 1 large tower overseeing the smaller ones. 108 is considered a sacred number in both Hindo and Buddishm. You can see Angkor Wat, Phnom Krom (South), Phnom Khulen (North) and Phnom Bok from the top, and sunrise and sunset views are splendid from here. There are two ways up to the top, with the side going up on the right, offering views of Prasat Baksei Chamkrong, and the West Baray.

In the afternoon, you can ride an elephant up for $20, and it takes about 15 minutes. The ride down is $15. I suggest you go up on the path that leads up to the right of the mountain, and come down on the one that leads up to the left of the mountain. The temple is very busy in the afternoon with people wanting to get a sunset view of Angkor Wat, although with most cameras you will not be able to see Angkor Wat. If you want the temple mostly to yourself to take splendid pictures of the countryside, come in the heat of the day at around noon.

Path up the mountain to the temple.

February 2014.

December 2014, restoration in progress.

Anton Swanepoel

Prasat Baksei Chamkrong

Date: Early to middle 10th century (rededicated in 948).
King: Harshavarman I, restored by Rajendravarman.
Religion: Hindu.
Style: Bakheng to Koh Ker.
Time: 20 minutes.
Best time to visit: Anytime for the temple, but during the morning to see the light to break through the treetops on the East side.
GPS: 13°25'30.9"N 103°51'33.6"E.

Prasat Baksei Chamkrong (the bird with sheltering wings) is a stepped pyramid temple, located 280m before the South Gate. The name however is new, and not relevant to the building of the temple. The temple fell into disarray, when the capital moved to Koh Ker, and was restored and rededicated in 948 by King Rajendravarman.

The temple has four tiers, that measure 27 x 27m at the base, to 15 x 15m at the top, with a 13m high tower that measures 8 x 8m at the base. The opening in the tower faces east. This temple is almost a smaller replicate to the main Koh Ker temple.

Steep steps on all four sides allow access to the top.

Date: Early 10th century.
King: Yasovarman I.
Religion: Hindu.
Style: Bakheng.
Time: 10 minutes.
GPS: 13°25'33.2"N 103°51'24.7"E.

Prasat Bei (the three towers) is a three-tower temple, on a single 24m x 10m laterite platform, which lies 300m down a dirt path along the moat of Angkor Thom City, 200m from the South Gate. The temple was unfinished, and later restored by Groslier in the later 1960s. The central tower contains a linga, with the central and south tower showing carvings of Indra on the elephant Airavata.

Just before going over the south bridge, take the dirt path to the left along the moat. The pick-up point for boat rides is currently just past this temple, and a stop here should be included if doing a boat ride.

Date: 10th century.
King: Yasovarman I.
Religion: Hindu.
Style: Bakheng
Time: 5 minutes.
GPS: 13°25'33.3"N 103°51'34.2"E.

Thma Bay Kaek (rock to place rice for the crows) is a small single structure, 190m before the South Gate, and right at the beginning of the South Bridge, on the left of the road.
A five-leaved gold treasure, arranged in a quincunx, with the central leaf carrying the image of Nandi (Shiva's bull) was found here. There is an archway and a stupa structure behind the temple. The archway structure has a linga in. This could possibly have been a prayer stupa, but details are not known.

Anton Swanepoel

Chapter 4: Siem Reap

Siem Reap town is the capital of Siem Reap province, and the closest town to the Angkor Archaeological Park. The town is the major hub for visits to the Angkor Wat Temple complex, and other temples as far as Preah Vihear, Koh Ker, and the Kulen Mountains. Following are temples and attractions, close to Siem Reap that are most visited, and includes the Roluos group temples, Beng Mealea, as well as Tonle Sap Lake, but not the Kulen Mountains, Koh Ker, or Kbal Spean, these attractions are listed under their own chapters.

Ak Yum Temple
Date: 7th ~ 8th century. Pre-Angkor.
Time: 15 minutes (includes drive from West Baray boat launch).
GPS: 13°25'29.3"N 103°46'36.5"E.
Entry Fee: None.

Ak Yum is Temple Mountain, about 900m from the boat pickup to West Mebon, on the same road. The temple is the oldest known Temple Mountain, however, exact dates are not known, nor who built it. Various inscriptions have been found at the temple, with the earliest dating to 609 and 674 on the main doorway, however, this piece was reused. The temple was used until the construction of the West Baray, where it was covered up, until discovered in 1932. An inscription dated early 11th century, reads that the temple was dedicated to Gamhiresvara (God of the Depths), a 7th century deity. Two Hindu and four Buddhists, bronze statues were found here.

The temple had a vault that led to a subterranean chamber that descended 12.5m down. Here a shrine with two elephant figures, and a 1.25m high statue of a man was found.

The temple is situated close to the road, (view looking back).

Looking down the hole where a shrine was.

Prasat Kamnap

Time: 5 minutes.
GPS: 13°26'26.5"N 103°56'08.8"E.
Entry Fee: None.

Prasat Kamnap's location is inside a Wat, on the way to Banteay Srei, on road 67, 280m from the road that leads out of the Angkor Park, on the right. However, nothing seems to remain of the temple. The view from the small bridge outside the Wat is actually interesting.

Banteay Samre

Date: Mid-12th century.
King: Suryavarman II, Yasovarman II.
Religion: Hindu.
Style: Angkor Wat.
Time: 1 hour (includes drive out).
Entry Fee: Angkor Pass.
Best time to visit: Early in the morning or late afternoon.
GPS: 13°26'33.5"N 103°57'32.6"E for temple.

Banteay Samre (the citadel of the Samre), is a smaller Angkor temple, situated 4.5km from the grand circuit road going through East Baray. The temple takes its name from the Samre people that inhabited the area.

Although the temple was dedicated to the Hindu God Vishnu, the lintels and pediments are richly decorated with Buddhist mythological scenes.

Locals tell of a Cucumber King legend associated with the temple. According to the legend, a farmer from the nearby village of Pradak, grew so tasty cucumbers, that the king ordered the farmer to kill anyone that tried to steal the cucumbers. One night the king wanted cucumbers so badly, that he went out himself to get some. The farmer did not recognize the king at night, and killed the king. As the king had no heir, a Royal elephant was decided upon to appoint the new king. The elephant went to the farmer, and knelt in front of the farmer, and the farmer became the new king. The old king was apparently buried at Pre Rup. The royal servants dislike the new king, and he fled to hide in Banteay Samre Temple.

To get to the temple, go along the grand circuit, and take road 810 to the right, 950m after Pre Rup. Follow this road for 4.1km, though Pradak village, and take the turn off to the temple, which is 250m down the side road.

Anton Swanepoel

Banteay Srei Temple / Citadel of the Women

Date: 967.
King: Yajnavarah (King Rajendravarman's counselor).
Religion: Hindu.
Style: Banteay Srei.
Time: 2 to 4 hours.
Entry Fee: Angkor Pass.
Gate Closes: 5pm.
Best time to visit: Early in the morning or late afternoon.
GPS: 13°35'52.6"N 103°57'56.7"E.

Banteay Srei (Citadel of the Women) / Tribhuvanamahesvra (Great Lord of the Threefold World), is situated 20km from where road 810 links up with the grand circuit road in the east baray (same road as going to Banteay Samre). Drive time is about 20 minutes. From town, the temple is 35km and normally takes 45 minutes with traffic.

The temple was built with red sandstone that coupled with the richly carved figures, makes this a must see temple, especially at sunrise or sunset as the sun's rays gives the temple a golden look (most people do sunset after seeing Angkor Wat). There are a number of Khmer shops and restaurants in the complex, as well as a more upmarket restaurant that sells very good food.

When you exit the temple complex at the back, you can turn right, and follow the road a short distance to an observation station. From here, the road continues along a very scenic area, and ends by a rest station than normally has water and drinks, as well as canoes that one can take a river ride in (about $5). Parking for cars and motorbikes are provided, at 1000 Riel.

As this temple is close to Kbal Spean, I suggest you do the two as a day trip. Either go early in the morning and see the temple first, or do Kbal Spean, then stop at Banteay Srei in the afternoon as the sun sets.

Note, there is no ticket office currently here or at Kbal Spean, and you need your Angkor Pass to see either, so do not forget to bring it along, as you will not be able to enter. There was a ticket office, but with the new picture id passes, this one was closed for the time being.

After passing an information center and a place where you can store your bags, you pass a number of market stalls, including a restroom.

Nice countryside as you walk towards the entry point of the temple.

Anton Swanepoel

After passing the entry checkpoint, you come to a causeway.

After passing the first causeway, you will come to a second causeway.

Finally, you come to the inner temple complex, surrounded by a moat. This is the end of the wet season. December 2014, 2:30pm.

Inner complex, taken from the back entrance. 2:30pm.

Back of the temple complex, surrounded by a moat. 2:40pm.

Anton Swanepoel

First viewing area after turning right on exiting the temple complex.

Second viewing area.

Anton Swanepoel

Beng Mealea 'Lotus Pond'

Date: Middle of the 12th century.
King: Suryavarman II.
Religion: Hindu.
Style: Angkor Wat.
Time: +4 hours (travel time is about 1 to 2 hours each way.)
GPS: 13°28'11.3"N 104°13'05.0"E for ticket office for Beng Mealea and Koh Ker temple.
GPS: 13°28'32.2"N 104°13'29.4"E Cool entrance.
GPS: 13°28'17.9"N 104°13'45.4"E Normal entrance.
Entry Fee: $5.

Beng Mealea is a partially restored temple, situated in a lush forest, 64km from Siem Reap town. Built out of large sandstone blocks, that are decorated with Hindu and Buddhist depictions, now mostly vine and moss covered, it is a must see. The temple is oriented east, and wooden stairs and pathways allow you to walk easily through the partially ruined complex. A Dharmasala (house of fire), is situated at the West terrace near the moat, and was used to shelter traveling pilgrims.

As the temple is so far from town, suggest doing Koh Ker in the morning, Beng Mealea on the way back, and possibly the Roluos Group if enough time remains. From the roundabout where national road 6 crosses Pokambor Ave (road going to Angkor), go 32.9km along road 6 until Damdek. At Damdek, turn left into a side road (13°14'41.6"N 104°07'22.4"E) (pass by the market), and continue for 31km. You will come to a ticket office just before the temple. Beng Mealea is currently $5, and Koh Ker is $8. Do get your ticket for Koh Ker here, as this is the only office.

Just after the ticket office, take the first left, and then enter the temple by the walkway a short distance down the road. This requires climbing over some large stones. For the normal entrance, carry on with the road after the ticket office, and the entrance will be on your left.

Turn at 13°28'16.3"N 104°13'28.1"E (just before the temple, the first road after ticket office) for cool entrance or to continue on to Koh Ker.

Anton Swanepoel

You need to go over the wall, to the left is easier.

Inside, go to the left, and look for an opening near the wall, then go under an archway, and up wooden stairs.

Anton Swanepoel

Anton Swanepoel

Phnom Bok

Date: 880.
King: Yasovarman I.
Religion: Hindu.
Style: Bakheng.
Time: 2 ~ 3 hours.
GPS: 13°27'56.2"N 103°59'02.4"E.
Entry Fee: None at time of writing.

Phnom Bok (the humped mountain) is 24km from Siem Reap central, and together with Phnom Bakheng and Phnom Krom, forms the trilogy of Temples Mountains. The complex has a Stupa, a pagoda, two artillery pieces, a rock carving, and five temple towers at the top. There is a staircase that consists of 635 steps, with an additional steep walk up to the top.

The view from the top is well worth the climb, but do pace yourself as it is a bit of an excursion.

From town, travel along national road 6, then turn onto road 67 as going to Banteay Srei (13°21'14.9"N 103°55'00.4"E). Keep going for 11.8km, then turn right into a side road at 13°27'23.3"N 103°56'15.8"E. Go for 4.8km until you come to a T-junction at 13°27'22.9"N 103°58'56.7"E, then turn left. Entrance is 500m further along on the left.

There are guards normally on station at Phnom Bok that will take you around on a tour, for a few dollars.

Do note that the climb is steep and it can get very hot. Bring or buy water at the Khmer shops for the walk up, and do take rest stops if you are not fit. There is a steep gravel path with loose rocks after the steps, thus walking or hiking shoes against flip-flops are recommended.

Note; see Prasat To as you go to this Temple. It is 5m down a side road, 1.8km from the turn off at road 67, on the 4.8km stretch of road to Phnom Bok.

Entrance to the complex.

Burial place.

Anton Swanepoel

The first artillery piece.

Pagoda on the top just before the temple towers.

A guard giving a tour.

The second artillery piece on the mountain.

A large rock that is considered sacred.

Phnom Krom

Date: Late 9th century.
King: Yasovarman I.
Religion: Hindu.
Style: Bakheng.
Time: ½ ~ 2 hours.
GPS: 13°17'10.8"N 103°49'12.2"E Bottom of staircase.
GPS: 13°17'00.1"N 103°48'59.8"E Start of road going up.
GPS: 13°17'08.0"N 103°48'43.9"E temple.
Entry Fee: Normally none, but an Angkor Pass may be required at random as it seems to be a hit and miss when a guard is on duty (mostly on festive and holiday, days).

Prasat Phnom Krom (the downstream mountain) sits on a 137m high mountain, 12.4 km from Siem Reap, on the road that leads to Tonle Sap Lake. The temple was dedicated to the Shiva, Vishnu, and Brahma. The temple consists of six towers that are aligned N-S, and is one of the three mountain temples, together with Phnom Bakheng and Phnom Bok, forms the trilogy of Temples Mountains.
The temple can be reached by a steep staircase, followed by a steep road, or by bypassing the steps and taking the road up. At the base of the mountain, where the road to go up starts, is a boat launch where one can at times hire a boat to go a short distance along the river. As this temple is a distance from town, and close to Tonle Sap Lake, it is suggested to do both on the same trip.

Stairs that lead part way up. From here, it is still a very steep climb to the top. If you come by Tuk Tuk and want to climb the stairs, have your driver meet you at the top of the stairs. There is a market to the left, at the bottom of the stairs. To bypass the steps, go 550m past the staircase, until you get a cement road leading up the mountain. The boat launch is directly opposite the road leading up.

You will pass a Pagoda as you go up.

There is a prayer area next to a rock, to the right if you go around before heading up.

Anton Swanepoel

Prasat To

Time: 5 minutes.
GPS: 13°27'24.5"N 103°57'15.2"E.

Prasat To is a temple in total ruin, except for an archway, and is on the road to Phnom Bok. As the temple is not of importance, it is rarely visited. Suggest stopping here if going to Phnom Bok. See Phnom Bok for direction to the temple.

Anton Swanepoel

Prasat To, archway.

Roluos group

The Roluos group (originally Hariharalaya), is a group of temples where King Indravarman I, built his first capital. There are a number of temples in the Roluos group; however, the following five temples are the most popular. These temples are often done as an ending to a trip to Beng Mealea, and sometimes to Koh Ker. Note, all temples except Prei Monti and Trapeang Kaek, require and Angkor Pass to enter.

Bakong Temple

Date: 881.
King: Indravarman I.
Religion: Hindu.
Style: Bakong.
Time: 1 hour.
GPS: 13°20'52.8"N 103°58'26.4"E turn off from national road 6.
GPS: 13°20'09.3"N 103°58'35.2"E for temple.
Entry Fee: Angkor Pass.

Bakong is a mountain temple, about 14.5km from Siem Reap, along national road 6 towards Phnom Penh. Bakong was the state temple of King Indravarman I, in the capital city King Jayavarman II used before he moved down from the Kulen Mountains. The temple complex measures 900m x 700m, and encloses two moats, with the base of the temple measuring 67m x 65m, and its stop area 20m x 18m.

The inner moat remains filled, and gives spectacular views as one approach the temple from the second turn off, from national road 6. A main attraction of the temple, besides, its size, is the lintels that contain intricate carvings of Naga's and Makara's. 22 brick temples in various states of collapse surround the main temple. A Naga Bridge that crosses the outer moat, has seven headed Naga snakes, on its sides, and is the first examples of a Naga bridge. There are two entry points to the complex, with the one suggested having a small tower close to the entrance.

To reach the complex, travel 12.5km from town, along national road 6 towards Phnom Penh. Take a side road where a signboard directs to the temple, then travel 1.1km down the road, past Preah Ko and the Angkor Miniatures, until you come to a T-junction. You can go either left or right around, both have entrances. To see the small temple near the entrance as mentioned before, go left around. The moat will be in front of you at the T-junction, with Bakong temple in the distance.

Note, if you want to see Prei Monti temple, then take the road off national road 6 immediately before this road, see Prei Monti for directions.

Moat with temple in the background when you come to the T-junction.

Temple structure outside and on the tip of a Y-split in the road, across the suggested entrance to Bakong temple. 13°20'06.7"N 103°58'34.6"E.

Inner moat on the right hand side as you walk to the temple.

Anton Swanepoel

One of the temple structures surrounding the temple.

Top tower, thought to possibly have been added by King Yasovarman I.

Preah Ko

Date: 879.
King: Indravarman I.
Religion: Hindu.
Style: Preah Ko.
Time: 20 ~ 30 minutes.
GPS: 13°20'52.8"N 103°58'26.4"E turn off from national road 6.
GPS: 13°20'38.0"N 103°58'26.1"E.
Entry Fee: Angkor Pass.

Preah Ko (the sacred bull (Nandin)), is located 650m before Bakong temple, on the same road. The temple was dedicated to Shiva, and named after the sacred bull Nandi. The temple is the oldest temple in the group, and was the first temple built by King Indravarman I. The temple, possibly included the Royal Palace, however, no trace of it has been found as of yet. The temple consists of six towers, on a single base, surrounded by an inner wall measuring 97m x 94m, and an outer wall measuring 500m x 400m.

Outer wall of the temple.

Lions guarding the entrance.

Do not forget to visit Angkor Miniatures across the road from this temple.

Anton Swanepoel

Prei Monti

Date: 9th Century.
King: Jayavarman III.
Religion: Hindu.
Time: 15 minutes.
GPS: 13°20'52.6"N 103°58'02.1"E for turn from national road 6.
GPS: 13°20'09.1"N 103°57'58.7"E for first turn.
GPS: 13°20'09.3"N 103°58'12.2"E for second turn.
GPS: 13°19'33.8"N 103°58'05.5"E for last turn.
GPS: 13°19'40.6"N 103°58'18.6"E for temple.
Entry Fee: None at current.

The road to this temple is 750m before the turn to Bakong temple, and right by a sign saying Vessvan Primary school. From the turn at national road 6, go 1.4km down the road, until you come to the first turn, turn left and go 400m down this road (the road leads also to Bakong temple). At the second turn, just before Bakong temple, go right. (There should be a signpost for the temple). Go 1.1km down the road, and look for a small road into the forest on your left, there should be a signpost here as well. This is the last turn, go left and 500m into the forest, the temple will be on the left side. The temple is rarely visited, but makes a good tour if you are on a bicycle or have your own motorcycle as it is in the forest.

Anton Swanepoel

Prasat Lolei

Date: 893.
King: Yasovarman I.
Religion: Hindu.
Style: Preah Ko ~ Bakheng.
Time: 15 minutes.
GPS: 13°21'08.6"N 103°58'29.4"E.
Entry Fee: Angkor Pass.

Prasat Lolei is an island temple, built on a 90m x 80m artificial island in the Indratataka baray, 1km from the turn off to Bakong temple. There are four towers in the complex, with a small garden and a pagoda. Khmer restaurants and shops are situated at the bottom of the island. To get to the temple, look for a signpost on the left, 400m after the Bakong turn as you are coming from Siem Reap and going to Phnom Penh.

Steps leading up to the temple.

Trapeang Kaek Temple

Date: 9th century.
King: Jayavarman III.
Religion: Hindu.
Time: 5 minutes.
GPS: 13°20'09.1"N 103°57'58.7"E for first turn.
GPS: 13°20'10.5"N 103°57'23.8"E for temple.

This single tower Prasat, is 2.7km from Prasat Bakong, right next to the road. Not much to see, but if you have time, give it a go. From national road 6, go as if going to Prasat Monti, but turn right at the first turn, then keep going for 1.1km.

Not much remains of the Prasat, and it is deteriorating more each year. However, with its historic importance, and ease to locate, it should be included in a visit to the Roluos group. If time is a problem, however, then Preah Monti temple is more rewarding, and it takes about the same time to reach either temple.

West Baray / Baray Toek Thla

Date: Beginning to middle of the 11th century.
King: Suryavarman I.
Time: 15 minutes.
GPS: 13°25'29.1"N 103°47'05.9"E for boat dock.

West Baray is 8km x 2.2km, and is the largest fabricated body of water at Angkor. It has an average depth of 7m, and holds around 123 million cubic liters of water. Even today, the baray is a major source of fish for the locals, as well as a spot to swim, picnic and relax. The baray water level drops by meters, between the dry and wet season. The boat dock to catch a boat out to West Mebon is situated 11.2km from Siem Reap central. From Siem Reap, head 8.3km along national road 6 towards the airport, then take a right into a side road just before a small bridge at the turn off listed (towards the paradise Eco resort). Travel an additional 3km along the road until you come to the baray wall.

Water channel running from the wall towards Siem Reap city.

Shops and Khmer restaurants close to the boat launch.

The baray in the dry season. February 2014.

Baray in the wet season, shops shifted to next to the wall. December 2014.

Boats at anchor in the dry season.

Anton Swanepoel

Boats at anchor in the wet season.

West Mebon

Date: Middle of the 11th century (1066).
King: Udayadityavarman II.
Religion: Hindu.
Style: Baphuon.
Time: 1 hour (includes boat trip).
GPS: 13°25'29.1"N 103°47'05.9"E for boat dock.
Price: Around $15 for the boat ride, (negotiate with the captain).

Prasat West Mebon is about 4km west of Angkor Thom, and situated on an artificial island, about 150m in diameter that is reached by boat. At the time of writing, it was not possible to reach the actual ruins, as it is fenced off for reconstruction. You can walk along the edge, but for the money to get here, at the time is not very rewarding. In the dry season, the boat cannot reach the island, and you need to wade through knee-deep water, and then make your way to the temple, the walk is about 10 to 15 minutes.

Boat at anchor, in the dry season.

Field as you walk to the temple, dry season.

Anton Swanepoel

Thank you for taking the time to read **Angkor Wat Archaeological Park**.

If you enjoyed this book or found it useful, I would be very grateful if you would please post a short review because your support really does make a difference. Alternatively, consider telling your friends about this book because word of mouth is an author's best friend and much appreciated.

Thank you very much for your time.

Anton Swanepoel

If you want to contact me personally, send me an email @ info@antonswanepoelbooks.com

Follow this link if you want updates on new book releases by me, as well as travel tips from my blog posts.
http://antonswanepoelbooks.com/subscribe.php

Chapter 5: Itinerary

The intention of this book is for you to view the pictures of the temples, and decide what temples you want to see for yourself. However, here are some suggestions if you are at a loss of what to see on a short time frame. Do know, that this suggestion is my own for the temples and places I think are nice, and will differ from guide to guide and tour group to group.

Angkor Park, Siem Reap and nearby Temples
Day 1:
Sunrise at Angkor Wat Temple, then view the reflection of the temple in one of the side pools in front of the temple, then head to the top tower. Head to the Elephant and Leper King terraces before 9:30 (preferably 8:30) to see the sun reflected on them, then see Baphuon temple, Phimeanakas temple and Royal pools, then head over to Bayon temple, then for a sunset head over to Phnom Bakheng while making a stop at the South Gate and a stop at Prasat Baksei Chamkrong.

Day 2:
Sunrise at Srah Srang, then head over to Ta Prohm (be there early to avoid the crowds), then head to Ta Keo followed by the Victory gate. View the North and South Khleang group as well as the Prasat Suor Prat and the Preah Pithu Group. Make it to Preah Khan by 2pm, then from there head to Ta Som, then do a sunset at Angkor Wat temple.

Day 3: Option A:
Sunrise at Banteay Srei temple, then see Banteay Samre, head to East Mebon, then to Neak Pean, go through the North Gate, then the Victory gate, and see Thommanon and Chao Say Tevoda, followed by any smaller temples of your liking.

Day 3: Option B:
Sunrise at Bakong temple in the Roluos group, then do Prei Monti and Preah Ko, followed by Banteay Samre, East Mebon, then to Neak Pean. If time allows, see Thommanon and Chao Say Tevoda, then a sunset at Banteay Srei. Do allow for about 25 minutes ride from inside Angkor Park to Banteay Srei.

Day 3: Option C:
Do a sunrise at Banteay Srei temple, then head over to Kbal Spean and do lunch here, then see Banteay Samre, then do Neak Pean, go through the North Gate, then the Victory gate, and see Thommanon and Chao Say Tevoda.

Day 4: Energetic
Whole day at Kulen mountains, be at the gate by 7am, and the waterfall by 7:45 to have no one around, then see the temple at the waterfall, followed by the leper king terrace, 1000 lingas, and natural spring, then go see the big Buddha and the footprint, followed by the Bat Cave and Krol Damrei temple site, and late afternoon at Preah Kral on top of Phnom Kulen. Note, it is possible (I have done it) to be very early at Kulen mountain, do a quick view of the waterfalls, and 1000 lingas, natural spring, with a short trip to the big Buddha and the top of Phnom Kulen, then race over to Kbal Spean, and do a sunset at Banteay Srei on the way back to town.

Day 5:
Head out to Koh Ker temple site, then return in time to see Beng Mealea. If you head out to be at Koh Ker when the gates opens, and come back by lunch time, you can see Chau Srei Vibol as well, or possibly do sunset at the Roluos group. You can also do Beng Mealea first, then the Koh Ker group, followed by if there is time, the Roluos Group. Note, there are no guards at Prei Monti and Trapeang Kaek Temple, so you can do these after 5pm just before the sun, sets.

Day 6:
Full day out to Preah Vihear Temple site, early start.

Day 7:
Full day out, very early start, or possibly overnight. Head out to Anlong Ven and do the sites there in any order.

Day 8:
Full day out, very early start. Either head out yourself with your own transport to Sambor Preikuk Temple Site, or take a bus to Kampong Thom, then rent a motorcycle or tuk tuk there to the site.

Day 9:

Sunrise at Phnom Krom, then Tone Sap Lake, followed by sunset at Phnom Bok.

Day 10:

Full day out to Banteay Chhmar.

Day 11:

See the Museum, war museum, landmine museum.

Day 12 onwards:

See any temples that you missed, including those of interest to you.

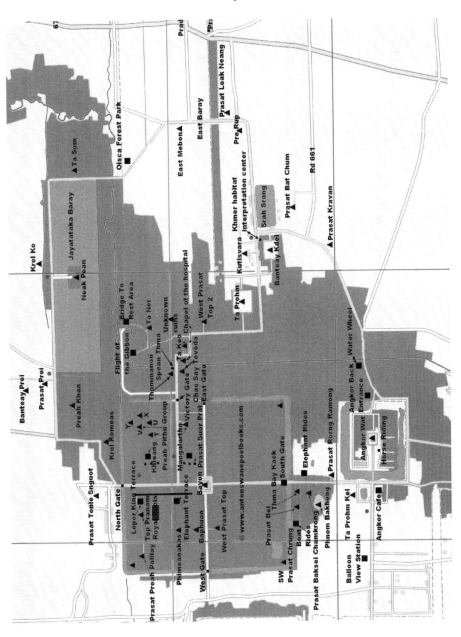

The map shown is a limited view of the Angkor Archaeological Park.

You can download a full view map. (Case sensitive URL).
Low resulotion (4mb)
http://www.antonswanepoelbooks.com/books/AntonSwanepoel/Angkor_Wat_Cambodia_Temples/Maps/Angkor_Map.jpg.

High resolution (10mb)
http://www.antonswanepoelbooks.com/books/AntonSwanepoel/Angkor_Wat_Cambodia_Temples/Maps/Angkor_Map_Large.jpg

You can also download a higher resolution of the limited map (**1mb**).
http://www.antonswanepoelbooks.com/books/AntonSwanepoel/Angkor_Wat_Cambodia_Temples/Maps/Angkor_Map_Limited.jpg

You may print the maps for personal use, but may not share or reuse the map, nor use it for any commercial purpose.

About the Author

Anton Swanepoel @ Pol Pot's house on the mountains in Thailand, and on his way to Preah Vihear Temple.

An ex software developer that left the corporate world, Anton for seven years worked as a technical diving instructor in the Cayman Islands. He is a Tri-Mix instructor for multiple agencies, and has dived to over 400ft on open circuit. While on Grand Cayman, he started his passion, writing, and currently has 20 books published.

In Jan 2014, Anton moved to Siem Reap, Cambodia, to go for his dream of being a full-time writer. Currently living cheaply off his savings, he loves to laugh, travel, and often worries too much.

Follow his adventures and share some laughs, tears, and moments of a lifetime. **www.antonswanepoelbooks.com/blog**.

More Books by Anton

www.antonswanepoelbooks.com

Novels
Laura and The Jaguar Prophecy (Book 1)
Laura and The God Code (Book 2)
Laura and the Spear of Destiny (Book 3)

Peru Travel
Machu Picchu: The Ultimate Guide to Machu Picchu

Travel Tips
Angkor Wat & Cambodia

Motorbike Travel
Motorcycle: A Guide Book To Long Distance And Adventure Riding
Motorbiking Cambodia & Vietnam

Cambodia Travel
Angkor Wat: 20 Must Ssee Temples
Angkor Wat Temples
Angkor Wat Archaeological Park
Angkor Wat & Cambodia Temples
Kampot, Kep and Sihanoukville
Kampot: 20 Must See Attractions
Battambang: 20 Must See Attractions
Phnom Penh: 20 Must See Attractions
Siem Reap: 20 Must See Attarctions
Dangerous Loads
Sihanoukville 20 must see attraions
Kep 10 Must See Attractions

Vietnam Travel
Vietnam Caves
Ha Long Bay
The Perfumed Pagoda
Phong Nha Caves

Thailand
Bangkok: 20 Must See Attractions
Ayutthaya: 20 Must See Attractions
The Great Buddha

Laos
Vientiane: 20 Must See Attractions

Diving Books
Dive Computers
Gas Blender Program
Deep and Safety Stops, and Gradient Factors
Diving Below 130 Feet
The Art of Gas Blending

Writing Books
Supercharge Your Book Description (Grab Attention and Enhance Sales)

Self Help Books
Ear Pain
Sea and Motion Sickness

Made in the USA
Middletown, DE
03 January 2016